The Thinking Tree

Advanced Language Arts for High School Students

Viking

Vocabulary Building Exercises & Creative Composition Through Historical Fiction

Written by Grant Fontenot
Illustrated by Tolik Trishkin
Design by Sarah Hobbs & Sarah Janisse Brown

Table of Contents:

Prologue	1
"The Decadence of the Vengeful"	3
"Navigating Aficionados"	15
Week One: "Tips and Tricks"	17
"Warmongers of Their Day"	41
Week Two: "Thereafter"	43
Story Journal: Asger	65
"Horns and Hygiene"	77
Week Three: "The Fab Four"	79
"Linguistic Alteration"	109
Week Four: "Tale of an Anglo"	111
Story Journal: Brothers	133
"The Toughest Norseman"	147
Week Five: "Journaling"	148
"Not Something to be Unsure About"	179
Week Six: "Final"	181
Story Journal: Your Story	203
"The Hills are Alive"	215
Week Seven: "Practice Perfects"	217
Conclusion	239
Journal	241
Definitions	263
Word List	281

PROLOGUE
"Life, Liberty, and the Pursuit of... Rhetoric!"

Enhancing your language efficiency through the art of rhetoric is an achievable task. It is not exclusive to the elect of a society, nor is it a trait known only by the wise or seemingly infallible. In fact, to smarten yourself in this area is not at all problematic. With proper application, the process has the possibility to actually be quite enjoyable. It doesn't necessarily require endless hours of research to get to your desired level of comprehension. Regardless of your prior delver in this particular subject, or lack thereof, it is never too late to get started.

Now, let me be clear about which section of rhetoric I am defining. I am not suggesting the act of composing specialized, persuasive speech with which one presents a figure of reasoning through the use of syllogisms. (Although, that is indeed a very large and explored branch of study and such a skill set is also very obtainable.) Rhetoric by nature is manifold, containing within itself a numerous and diverse assortment of constituents. The component we will be most often exploring is that which pertains to prose. Our focus will be on learning to edify the listener or reader with a beautiful and stylistic word set. It will not be for the undue usage of bombast; for such a thing is injurious to any who will lend their precious time to listen to it.

The art of language has been modeled for us throughout the ages by countless Greek and Latin speaking philosophers and even by the bishops of the early Catholic Church. However, not every example is what we would call "shining". Many have sought for an occasion to use it as a means to peacock their affluent wellspring of education upon the neophytes of their day and age, as well as to impress colleagues. Its purpose, I'm sure, was to put on display an alluring outward aesthetic even if the content of their ideology was considered, by certain others to be, in reality, purely detrimental balderdash. Hopefully, this brief study in language will spur you on to greater degrees of thought.

It is my wish that you might feel inspired enough to continue educating yourself long after your time with this book is finished. My purpose is rather to teach a man to fish, than to catch the fish for him. I understand, entirely, that not all minds were built in the same fashion. All the same, you may rise or fall linguistically. Vocabulary and grammar are some of the fundamental pillars of our everyday lives. Quite truthfully, if you desire to obtain understanding, you will. We are, after all, living in the day of knowledge, where all the information necessary for our daily lives can easily be accumulated in mere moments. Therefore, you don't *need* me to tell you anything! But perhaps, you just need a nudge in the right direction.

IMPORTANT: Things you will need for this course!

1. A pack or two of index cards — You will be writing vocabulary words on them to make flashcards. (There are 150+ words.)
2. Dictionary
3. Lined paper or a digital writing program — In case you run out of space in this book or want to type your work.
4. Pencils and pens
5. Thesaurus

VIKING

"The Decadence of the Vengeful"

"There I stood, Asger (war chief of the Vikings), contending valiantly upon the field of battle!", a man well into his fifties elaborated. Before him sat a multitude of young men.

"Full of pride was I. Four and a half arm spans in length with a magnificently long, red beard flowing down my gritty face! The rest of my comrades and I had just about taken the entire town. Although, unbeknownst to those I led, my intentions were quite opposite theirs. I deviated from the chaos to seek out a former friend of mine.

He was my brother. I say 'was' for I had long since disowned him. In fact, my hatred for him grew in intensity by the day. His extermination was now long overdue. You may say I am being a bit extreme; however, you were not there when he savagely slew our master before my very eyes. Not only was this man my flesh and blood, but during our time away from one another, he managed to gain the rank of king over the people we had come to conquer.

So, on I went stealing toward the castle mount amidst all of the clamor and madness. The strength of most would have been taxed if they had undergone the same journey I did. But, there was kindled within me a high level of stamina, which pulsated throughout my entire body. I broke the line of defense by sheer frenzy.

Once I reached the fortress, I inferred the gate to be impregnable as it was constituted of thick wood. I paused for a moment to gather my bearings. I decided it best that I should ascend the outer wall. The sky was my limit; I felt no fear! With each second I spent climbing, my anger became all the greater, and my desire for revenge seemed all the more justifiable. I gained entrance through one of the turret windows. There were few men within the fortress halls for most everyone was out defending their homeland. Not a soul should have suspected an ambush on their commander and chief. With as strong and skilled a man as he was, any who opposed him were deemed foolish and wanting of death. In which case, you may call me the greatest fool to ever live! You see, both he and I were raised in the frigid outskirts of the Scandinavian Mountains. Trained and brought up by a bear-like man, we quickly found out that it was, either, learn fast, or die young. There was little room for anything other than a stalwart lifestyle. It was because of a bitter and resentful heart that my brother ambushed our master and slew him whilst his back was turned.

My progression towards his chamber was abruptly stunned when, along my path, I was met by one I knew well. It was Calder, a highly esteemed captain of my forces. In his hand he clutched a longbow and along his belt line he bared an assortment of various throwing knives. He was a nimble man of short beard, yet tougher than the rest of them. I have fought many wars alongside him; truly my most trusted partisan.

His face held a grimace, but beneath his cold expression, I could see the relief he had to find his master still alive. He spoke to me with an inquisitive and prying tongue, "Asger, my captain, why is it I find you in such a dismal place? You have gone astray from leading your forces. I watched as you climbed these very walls; it was then that I followed suit. Never before have I seen this look in your eyes. It is as a mad man's! Expose to me your intentions so that I might not presume incorrectly. What is it you seek? It could not possibly be for mere frivolity. You are not so unwise as to risk your life for naught. It could not be for wealth or for fame. For, if it were so, would you not be fighting alongside the rest of your countrymen? No, I am afraid you are withholding secrets from me. Tell me I am wrong, that I may dismiss all my doubts."

I thought it best that I disclose to him the entire truth. "Calder, long have I called you my servant, yet now I call you my friend. A friend such as you should understand my doings and be my advocate. Know now that I have been vexed, for what seems an eternity, by both the living and the dead. The hopelessness of my situation is that I will never obtain what I truly seek. Regaining my fallen master is a childish dream. I'm afraid the gods have seen fit to defer reviv-ing him even though I have sought it with many supplications. So then, let the dead bury their dead, I will continue on nonetheless. But, a scale I must balance, and an eye must I take for the eye he took from me. Follow if you must, but I warn you, should you stand between me and my vengeance, you will not stand long."

Calder understood my pain and wanted nothing more than to be my support. "Speak no more, my lord, for I apprehend your sorrow well. I, myself, have gathered riches galore and have fought countless battles. Yet, never have I fought for a cause nobler than this. Allow me to remind you of the pact I once made." After these words, he knelt down on one knee and, taking his bow, he leaned upon it as one does a sword. Drawing his breath, he spoke, "What you think, I will think. How you move, I will move. If you should be slain, I will avenge seven-fold. Now then, what does my lord have for me to do?"

With the increased size of my company, victory was inevitable. There, at the mouth of the throne room, we made our presence known through blatancy, not at all slowing down our stride to plan a well thought out stratagem. We, instead, relied heavily upon spontaneity. You can imagine how disheartened we were when, after barging through the doors, we found the room deserted. The king had fled along with the rest of the castle inhabitants. Gathering our senses, after an obvious large blow to our pride, we concluded that he could not possibly be far off. I groaned in my yearning, anxiously searching the surrounding rooms for a sign of his whereabouts.

Now, had Calder not been there that day, I would have truly been at a loss. He was, in fact, an excellent tracker and, with a keen eye, he caught sight of the enemy from a long distance. They were in the process of boarding one of their ships. Among them was, none other than, my brother himself, proud as he possibly could be. I will never forget the sight of his sails, ominously blood red, embroidered with the image of a dragon. He stared in our direction long enough for me to realize he knew exactly where I was. Overtaken with intense rage, I took action before Calder could give me sound counsel. Acting out of impulse, I jumped out the castle window.

While launching toward the earth at excessively high speeds, I had a few moments to think about my life up to that point. Perhaps I found myself in that sort of position far too often. There was little occasion, though, to dwell on past impudence; it was now time to react. With a stroke of luck, I landed on the slant of one of the rooves. Although, not without a great deal of pain. Gravity definitely had its way with me. Conveniently, near where I landed was a giant ax. I quickly judged it to be a sufficient weapon for my usage. Dazed, yet not delayed, it was easy to gather my speed again.

The outskirts of the castle were just as terrible a sight as one would imagine. Enemies and allies alike lay gracelessly across the war-torn ground. With a slight limp, I pursued to finish this once and for all. Every by-standing ally watched on in, what I'm sure was, great confusion. They no doubt had a few questions about where their captain had been all this time. Down an alley and across a field I dashed. All persons and problems seemed trivial and trite in comparison to the mission at hand. The ship was now a short distance at sea, yet not so far off that I could not reach them. He and I held eye contact as the distance was closed. My grip was tight around the ax handle and, in a flash, I released my hold to send it flying. My aim was precise, not an inch off. Yet, to my astonishment, (as if my day could not possibly become any worse) the weapon never met its mark. The great warrior dodged to the right and the blade plunged into the main mast. I could do nothing more. We had landed our long boats too far away. Therefore, pursuit was impossible. I fell to my knees and, with no desire to accomplish anything else, I was left to once again stew inside of my bitterness. Just then, behind me, I heard an all too familiar sound. It was the twang of a longbow. What followed was a sight I never thought I would witness. It was an arrow making its way speedily upon the runaway, lodging itself deep within his chest. Calder was, in the end, faithful to his word. The healing power of restoration began to work on my soul as the pain of my past slowly became abated.

That was the last I ever saw of my brother, and I believe it is the last I ever will." Asger ended the story with triumph. Yet, something in his eyes betrayed the excitement he held in his voice. He was an old man now, not nearly the warrior he once was. Whenever he spoke of his brother, there was inside of him something that wished things would have ended differently. Leaving the men with a heavy heart, Asger walked slowly to the water's edge. Nearby, the ships lay dormant. He allowed his eyes to drift lazily upon the far horizon. The sun was just about set. He then saw something which made his blood freeze solid.

"Red sails!" he cried out, "The Anglos are coming". He retreated to gain the attention of the city. One thing that went through his mind was whether his brother was truly dead or if there was perhaps a different ending to this tale after all? The boats were almost upon them now, and Asger was undoubtedly sure his brother was on board. The only question remaining was whether he was there for peace or for war?

"Navigating Aficionados"
The Genius of Earlier Times

Vikings were, above all the other tribes of their day, renowned sailors. They were known for their unique advantage in the realm of marine warfare. There was a manifold of different designs used for their ships in the area of aesthetics. Large wooden dragon heads would be placed on the front of their ships, which acquired them the name of *Dragon Boats*. Various colors coated each of their ships. This was possibly a method used to make themselves appear more intimidating. A spine was built on the underside of each boat, which gave it greater maneuverability and the buoyancy to float as much above the water as possible. Because of the ship's architecture, beach landings were not at all problematic.

Week One: "Tips and Tricks"
A Few Days on Grammar

    Before you get started on rhetoric, you must have a firm foundation. Now, I do not mean the bare necessities. This course is for those who are well enough acquainted with the basics to continue without strong difficulty. There are certain elements of the English language which are seldom heard in everyday speech, yet are paramount for most all formal writing styles. Let's just say, for now, that English is nowhere near to what it once was. How you text your buddies and write your memes make for a sad representation of where we are intellectually as a culture. That is, obviously, not meant to say that you (or anyone else) are not intelligent. In fact, I believe, we as humans have the capacity to be far more perceptive than we give ourselves credit for. I simply mean that the aspects of our language are diminishing. We have morphed into a society that contains nothing more than fast food slang, where enough to get by is all that is needed. Let's take a look at one of my personal favorites. It's a pronoun that would do you well to master.

Day One: "The Forgotten Stepsister"
A Lecture on Whom and the Objective

The conundrum, that has bewildered a countless many, has been held on by its fingertips alone. Thankfully, it has not become entirely obsolete. There are still many today who will take time to quicken their comprehension of its meaning. The word *whom* is the objective (accusative) form of the word *who*. Now, what that means is that there is a right way and a wrong way to use it.

The correct way is a lot simpler than most would suppose. *Whom* behaves exactly as *him*, *her*, *me*, *us* and *them* does. Many would suggest that, in your configuring of whether a certain situation calls for *whom* or not, you mentally substitute the other objective pronouns to see if they would be appropriate as well. That is an acceptable exercise; although, I would rather you learn by constant practice. After all, repetition is the mother of learning and skill. So then, if you would allow me the opportunity, I will give you the following sentences. Instead of me telling you the reason behind the madness, deduce it for yourself. Afterwards, I will inform you of its meaning.

Of whom much was given, much was required.
For whom are you speaking? Yourself or another?
They interviewed the one whom I gave an abundance of gifts to.
It was said in the presence of whom?
Within whom there is division of spirit, there is also unrest.
Go with whomever you wish. It makes no difference now.

So, have you deciphered the code? Do you believe it possible that you could do the same? I'll let you in on the secret.

Try this example: Who is killing whom?

Being connected to the verb, *is* gives who the ability to be who. Being the object of the killing is causing whom to be whom. You could also say who killed whom? Even without the is, it would be the same because of killed. So then, who (being the subject) enacted its vengeance upon their ugly stepsister, whom. I am not sure why they would do such a thing. I suppose though that they were probably jealous of her.

Not only is the verb a means to tell which pronoun is appropriate, there are other ways too. Take any preposition you can think of. It could be *to*, *for*, *with*, *between*, *of*, *aboard*, *before*, *about*, *from*, *above*, *opposite*, *across*, *under*, *etc*. For example, place a preposition at the beginning of your sentence. Then place the word *whom* right after the preposition. Now add an ending to your sentence and then you have a correct sentence. The same can be done for both the preposition and the pronoun at the end of the sentence. The preposition also, does not have to be at the beginning. It can go directly after the verb or noun. For instance:

> Whom knowledge was given to constantly.
> Whom we gave knowledge to constantly.

So, that's it for my lesson on the usage of whom. It is possible that this is not the only way you are able to use it. What comes next is you writing some sentences of your own.

VOCABULARY: None today.

CHALLENGE: Your mission, should you choose to accept it, is to write ten separate short entries.

    a) Make a subject and an object.
    b) You must use whom in each.
    c) Your entries can be any number of sentences you choose.
    d) All they must contain is one full thought.

viking

Day Two: "You Are What You Read!"
A Lecture on Bad Habits

You might agree with my theory. After all, I am highly certain that I'm not the only one who holds it. It's the belief that the best way to learn vocabulary is to read good material. Truly, you become what you consume. If you only read books for five year olds, then you will start to write like it is for a five year old. If you read books meant for adults, then you will begin to write for an older audience. Any who believe they have a gift for writing, yet do not pursue it, may think themselves of a degree which they are not. They are not able to consistently make something of true value, let alone be able to go against anyone competitively. It may be that they are just too lazy to do the leg work necessary to get anywhere. But when one gives a rip, (this applies to anything in life, not just writing) they will be zealous in their passion. They will refine their so-called gift. They will, most likely, ardently confront hardships and place themselves in the way of certain other skillful individuals. They do this so that they might learn, be challenged, and not reside in a harbor of comfortability. This is crucial for anyone that wants to get anywhere in anything.

If we are to take upon ourselves this sort of attack strategy in life though, it would mean that we are not to oblige the laziness of our human nature. Not even for a second! We should not strive for anything other than gold. There should be sweat droplets and tears behind the "job well done". We should not be marked as a quasi-hard working, lazy lay-about who pumps out papers at a moment's notice to please whatever assignment we have been given.

So, I regard now rhetoric. What do you read? How do you speak? Do your text messages attain to an ungodly, superfluous amount of shorthand? I ask this so that you might take into account any bad habits you may have developed over time. Such habits have the possibility of impeding your progression as a student of rhetoric. It is of the utmost importance that you allow not even the slightest bit of leeway. Otherwise, you will notice that higher levels of linguistic endeavors will eventually become entirely impossible. I highly recommend that you be consistently reading good literature. Not just simple story books. (Although, there is absolutely nothing wrong with reading them in and of themselves.) It would be beneficial for you to also try to go above your grade level. It will, hopefully, cause you to be befuddled and give you reasons to look up anything you have not yet learned. This is how we grow.

It is now time for the rubber to hit the road. As you sift through the recesses of your mind in order to find what your largest snare is, you might recall certain things on which you should definitely improve. This is a chance to test yourself, not only to see where you are currently, but also where you want to be.

Take, for instance, the words below (those in bold). You may recognize them. They are the first five vocabulary words in our story about the Viking lord, Asger. They are also the first this course will consider.

VOCABULARY: (You will follow these instructions every day for the rest of the course.)
- a) Go to the back of this book, find each of today's words, and write their definitions there.
- b) Make a flashcard for each word you do not already know.
  - i) Write the word on one side of the card and the definition on the other.
- c) Every day's warm-ups will utilize all of that day's words. Some days will have you use them differently than others, but you will use the entire day's set each day.

Contend
Elaborate
Magnificent
Multitude
Valiant

CHALLENGE: Today's task is to write a truncated short story using each of the vocabulary words.
- a) Each word must be used in context.
- b) You only need to write for as long as it takes to use them all.
- c) Use whom at least once in your story.
- d) You are not confined to using the words in the forms they were given.
  - I.e. Contend can also be contending or contended.
- e) You can't copy what I've already written. (No short cuts!)

viking

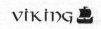

Viking

Day Three: "Repetitiveness Distracts"
A Lecture on Synonyms

One habit, that has the capability to negate and place a drag on your story, is when you repeat words. What that means is that settling for the same noun, verb, or adjective whenever you are talking about specific objects is oftentimes a killer of otherwise great stories. I know, personally, that this is one aspect that turns me off whenever I read any sort of text. That's not to say that you can't ever repeat anything at all. Be conscientious though, as it does have the possibility of being injurious to the point you are trying to bring across. Some important tools to have with you always are the thesaurus and the dictionary. The most useful type, is one that you find online. You can not only see the definitions, but the etymologies also, which show various other forms of the word you are wanting to use, examples of how the word is used, and much more.

Synonyms will be your main way of gaining a large vocabulary. If you see the possibility for a better word, but can't think for yourself what to put in its place, then don't feel ashamed to look it up in your thesaurus. Always make sure, though, that the words you are using are apropos and match well with what you are saying. Do this by looking up the new word in the dictionary as well. Once you are done writing, look back and reread it to get a good look at each and every word you used. That way, you will not only get the dictionary definition, but the context will be further ingrained in your memory. You could even read it out loud so that you, not only train your thinking skills, but your speaking skills as well.

Example:

- At that moment, it was *imperative* that I should give her up.
- After all, she was the *essential* reason for my many failures.
- There was nothing more to really say about it, but I knew then, without a shadow of a doubt, it was absolutely necessary.

Do you see what I did there? The first sentence contained the vocabulary word imperative. The second and third contained essential and necessary. All were synonyms of each other.

Imagine if I wrote it this way:

- At that moment, it was *imperative* that I should give her up.
- After all, she was the *imperative* reason for my many failures.
- There was nothing more to really say about it, I knew then, without a shadow of a doubt, it was absolutely imperative."

It doesn't really sound right, does it? You can't be sensible if you are constantly reiterating yourself this way. This is an extreme example, yes, but the same can happen with basically any word that is not an article, a preposition, a connecting verb, etc. (Even with those, you need to be careful not to repeat too often in sequence). Synonyms are key, not only to good writing, but to help the reader be challenged by discovering new words as well. It is now your turn to do the same. I suggest it best that you look up and choose your words before you write, instead of guessing their meaning and contextual accuracy. Unless, of course, you have an endlessly long lexicon within that so-called steel trap of yours.

VOCABULARY:
- Chaos
- Deviate
- Flow
- Former
- Unbeknownst

CHALLENGE: Write separate short entries, three sentences each, for all of today's vocabulary words.

a) The first sentence of each entry must contain one the given vocabulary words.

b) The following two sentences of each entry must contain a synonym of the first vocabulary word used.

c) Use no more than three sentences for each entry.

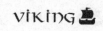

viking

Day Four: "It Is I"
A Lecture on the Subjective

Often forgotten and hardly used is the other half of the subjective case (also called nominative). We, for the most part, do not even know what the subjective case is (not that it's entirely necessary to). Its propriety has become archaic, when it should be standard. During my time abroad, I have heard an innumerable amount of other languages. A few of which I have studied to the extent of knowing at least a small portion. These languages seem to have kept this case intact, which caused me to wonder how and when we as language bearers determined it admissible to give it up.

The subjective case contains *I*, *you*, *he*, *she*, *it*, *we*, *they,* and *who*. We, for the most part, use these words correctly. Although, we have mistaken syntactical placement to mean the difference between cases; such should not the case (yes, I made a pun). The pronoun is connected to the verb, not to where it is in the sentence.

For instance: *This is she.* and *It is he.,* are both correct sentences and are often preferred over their modernized variables. They have been altered into things such as *this is her* and *it's him.* Now, to you and many others, the latter example may seem like correct grammar. However, the pronoun is still connected to the verb regardless of whether it's at the beginning of the sentence or at the end. Also, the subjective case (although many do not know it) is used for comparatives, which means it follows *like or as*. Sentences like *She is greater than I.* and *They did the same as she.* are also correct, as opposed to *She is greater than me.* and *They did the same as her.* As I have stated in an earlier lesson, the objectives *me*, *him*, *her*, *us*, *them*, and *whom* should only be used when the pronoun is in the *objective* case, which can be indicated by either its relationship to the subject or by a preposition.

In today's culture, it is not necessary that you speak like this (although some would definitely be impressed if you did). The standard is low, and you might as well just condescend to those around you. But, if you are writing formally, it is required so that you do not, at the very least, sound like a complete Neanderthal.

One thing that has been debated is whether to use he and I instead of me and him when used in the context of the subject doing something. To which I say, "If it is not appropriate for you to say me went and did this then why would it be alright to say me and him went and did this?" Not everyone understands where I am coming from. I assume, though, they have had it ingrained into their heads for so long, that they are just unable to grasp anything else. Let's hope you are not the same. Just know that she, he and I picked apples sounds far better than me, him and her were eating. Saying two objective cases (me and him) is only appropriate when it's objective. I know it's crazy how it works like that. (You must forgive my facetiousness. You would not believe the amount of arguments and/or explanations I have had about this exact sort of thing.)

VOCABULARY:

Disown
Extermination
Extreme
Intense

Repetition is the mother of learning. Work on your flashcards and memorization.

CHALLENGE: The assignment for today is to take everything we have looked at in this previous week and, incorporate it with today's five vocabulary words.

a) Use whom at least once.
b) Use as many synonyms as is relevant to your entry.
c) Use the subjective case at least twice while following like or as.

Day Five: "As for Similes"
A Short Lecture on Likening

Useful literary devices to add to your arsenal are the simile and the metaphor. The Bible uses both of these all throughout scripture. Take for instance, the book of Revelation where John had never before seen any of the things that God was showing him. He was forced to describe the things he saw as being *like* something, or it *was* something. What the simile does is compare one thing to another by saying that it is *like* the other object. You can also say that an object is *as* something else.

Examples:
The graceful doe skips *like* the gentle water brook.
Or... The horde of dragons voraciously devoured the men *as* if they were dogs who had gone weeks without sustenance.

So whether you are talking about a tender deer or about hungry reptiles, the rule is the same. *Like* and *as* are used to compare two separate objects. This is the simile.

How the metaphor works is slightly different. Instead of saying *like* or *as*, you just say that something *is* something else.

Example: The man was a stalwart bear in the fighting ring.

The man was not literally a bear, but he performed as one does. Using metaphors is a tremendous way to boost your story telling and should be considered something worth exploring. You don't necessarily have to only use an adjective to describe something. Instead, next time, try likening your object to something else. You might be surprised at your result.

VOCABULARY:
Amidst
Clamor
Slay

Don't forget your flashcards. They are for your benefit.

CHALLENGE: Use both the metaphor and the simile with today's vocabulary.
a) A separate entry for each word must be written.
b) Make three entries using one vocabulary word each and containing similes.
c) Make three entries using one vocabulary word each and containing metaphors.

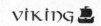

"WARMONGERS OF THEIR DAY" TO WAR OR NOT TO WAR?

Viking castles were armed to the tooth with defenses. Not only were they steep, and seemingly impenetrable in and of themselves, but the people which defended the castle were a force to be reckoned with indeed! From what we have to look at today, it appears that the Vikings were experts in all things warlike, from being deathly accurate with the bow, to being equally killer with the sword. Not easily was a castle taken. It would take some guts (and possibly someone with a long time grudge) to even consider trying to attack one, let alone climb it! Small sockets called murder, near the front gate, were supposedly used to pour boiling oil on those who tried a direct attack. Tall turrets concealed archers who were ready and willing to fire upon all. To top it all off, a moat usually surrounded the whole thing, giving it the utmost advantage in almost any foreseen strike.

Week Two: "Thereafter"
The Resolution

The intent of this course is to refine the skills you already have. My desire is to be the catalyst that takes your rich talent and abound it ever onward. The following week will not contain me yakking away about various writing tips and things I think crucial for your success. You need only to follow certain guidelines I have set out.

Each day you will have three sections:

1. **Vocabulary:** Just like before, you will daily find and add the word's definitions to the end of this book, and make flashcards for the words you don't know so that you can study them.

2. **Warm-ups:** These are exercises that will help you to further develop and strengthen your writing abilities.

3. **Challenge:** This week, you will be writing a one page story containing the events that follow Asger seeing his brother again. When you read it the first time, did you think it strange that it was left at such a cliffhanger? That was intended. You see, it was my objective all along that you finish the story yourself. The ending is still unknown and undecided. It will be your honor this week to create whatever it is you want to have happen.

    a) All you need to do is fill out one full page. It can be written in the end of this week's section, on paper from a different source, or in a word document on your computer or tablet. What you write it on doesn't matter, just that it is one full standard page size.

    b) You do not have to stop at one page either. That is all that is needed to complete the challenge, but you can write more.

    c) After each day's information, you'll be given a few pages to do your warm-ups. At the end of this week's section, you'll find a set of journal pages where you can work on your story.

Day Six:
"Begin with Some Push-Ups"

VOCABULARY: Figure out a way to incorporate all the words into your warm-ups. You should also continue to fill in the definition for each day's words in the back of the book, and make your flashcards daily.

Frenzy
Kindle
Pulsate
Sheer
Stamina

WARM-UPS: There are a few pages for you to write.
- a) Write three sentences. Use whom at least once.
- b) Write four sentences.
    - i.) Use the initial vocabulary word of your choice in the first.
    - ii.) Then, use different synonyms for the following three sentences.
- c) Write three sentences using two subjects in at least one of them.
Example: He and I went to the monster truck rally.
- d) Write two sentences using at least one simile.
- e) Write two sentences using at least one metaphor.

CHALLENGE: Now that you are done warming up, you should get started on your story of Asger. Begin where I left off. If you need to, reread it to get a better grasp on what you want to do.

viking

Day Seven:
"Manifold Warm-ups"

VOCABULARY: Use the following words within the warm-ups.

Ascend
Bearing
Impregnable
Infer

WARM-UPS:
- a) Write three sentences. Use whom at least once.
- b) Write four sentences. Use the initial vocabulary word of your choice in the first sentence and then synonyms for the following sentences.
- c) Write three sentences using two subjects in each of them.

   Example: She and I enjoy holding hands while frolicking through the luscious meadow.

- d) Write two sentences using at least one simile.
- e) Write two sentences using at least one metaphor.

CHALLENGE: After finishing these off, continue with your story on the Viking. A good thing to have is an extra pair of eyes. Although yours may be sharp and able to grab any and all discrepancies, it is still important that someone else checks your work. After you are done with a section of writing, make sure to go back and look at everything you have done. Edit the guts out of your paper if you have to.

Day Eight:
"Can I Have the Time, Sir?"

VOCABULARY:

    Ambush
    Intensity
    Justifiable
    Skilled

WARM-UP: Write a twelve to seventeen sentence story about a man that has lost his pocket watch.
- a) It must contain all the Vocabulary Words.
- b) It must have whom at least once.
- c) There must be either a metaphor or a simile used somewhere within.
- d) Feel free to use as many synonyms as possible.
- e) At least one subject and subject or object and object.
- f) Feel free to edit it as much as you like.

CHALLENGE: Continue working on your Asger story.

                Off to writing for you! Enjoy.

Day Nine:
"Of Windows, Trees, and Desks"

VOCABULARY:
    Deem
    Foolish
    Oppose

WARM-UP: Set a timer and write for 10 minutes about either something on your desk, something you see outside your window, or about the last book you read.

    a)   Include all of today's vocabulary words.
    b)   Do it without editing and without looking at the clock.
          i.)   I know this is difficult, I am not even able to do this without doing at least a little editing. If you succeed though, it's very beneficial, so do your best.

CHALLENGE: Now, today should be the day that you finish writing your story on Asger. Tomorrow will be all about editing it. Today, though, should be the end of your writing.

Day Ten:
"One Final Edit"

So, I do anticipate that at this point you have achieved a level of perfection with your story. That's not to say that any story is necessarily ever "perfect" in our eyes. To us writers, there is almost always something that can be better. We say things in our mind such as, "Oh, I don't like this" or, "I should change this". Even with the story I wrote on Asger, I do not see it as impeccable or without blemish and I say that having edited it more times than I can count. It was my first full length short story. I had to come to grips with the fact that there comes a time when you have to say, "enough is enough", and let it lie. In fact, the version you see is not my first attempt, it is my second. The first one was much too pretentious and bombastic to release to the public. But I digress, today will be reserved for you to edit your story, (if indeed you have finished it). Remember, there comes a time when you need to just let it rest. Next time you write a short story, (or, perhaps, later down the road when you happen to rewrite this one) you will have more of an idea of what you want to say. Our minds sharpen with use over time, not with just sitting around. I do not care if someone says they are a natural writer, yet have nothing to show. Writing is 1% talent and 99% practice. Getting your hands dirty is the only thing that will get you to a higher caliber, not believing you are something you are not.

VOCABULARY: Don't forget to write down the definitions in the back of the book, to make your flashcards, and to practice your vocabulary cards.

    Abrupt
    Bitter
    Progression
    Stalwart

WARM-UPS:
    a)   Take each of today's words and use them in three separate sentences.
    b)   None of the sentences can have any correlation to the others.
    Examples:
    i.) The way she strut her stuff was far too ostentatious for my liking.
    ii.) I have noticed that, on average, those who come from a life of privilege tend to come across as gaudy and ostentatious.
    iii.) The **NFL** has become so ostentatious, in fact, that most people see it as the only reason they are still in business.

CHALLENGE: Once you are finished with the warm-ups, it's time to finish up, and edit your story. Read through your story. Find and correct any spelling, grammar, and punctuation mistakes. Then, if you are writing by hand, rewrite your story on fresh paper, including the corrections. There will be more opportunities to write, so don't be dismayed if it isn't all you had hoped for.

viking

STORY JOURNAL

Here are some pages to use to work on your Asger story. The last couple of pages are there for you to rewrite your story after you have finished writing and editing it.

VIKING

viking

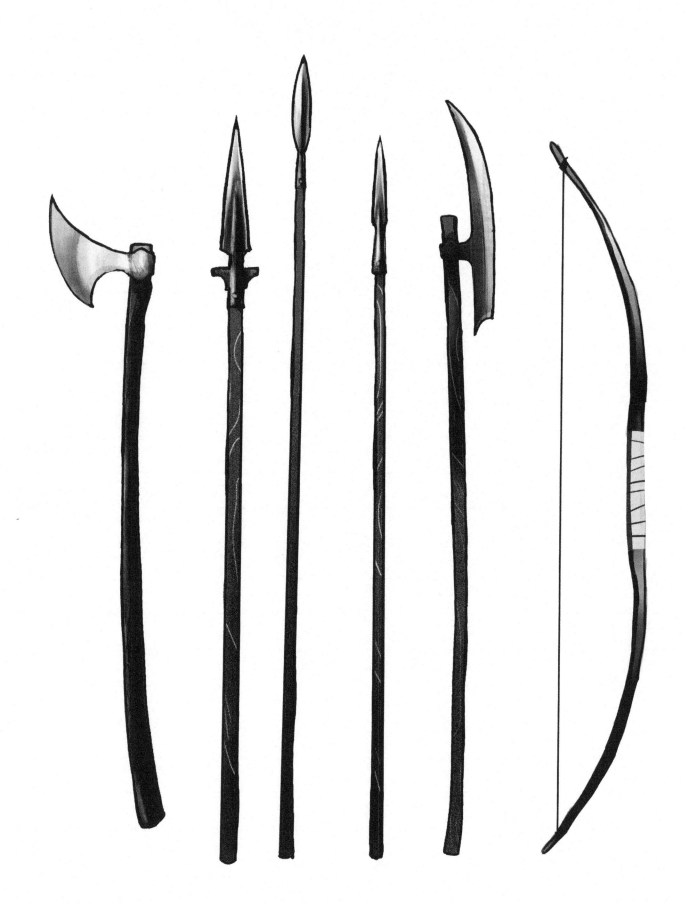

"HORNS AND HYGIENE" TO EXPOSE VIKING MYTH

This might be news for you, but the Vikings were actually incredibly well kept. Archeological digs have discovered combs, razors, and many other hygienic maintenance tools all throughout their civilizations. I'm not sure what you think about when you think of a Viking, but I tend to think of them as a bunch of ruffians running around with horns on their heads being about as disgusting as can be! Also a fun fact, Vikings never even wore the famed horn helmets we have all come to know and love. It is only a myth. Painters in the 19th century seem to have spurred it on with their depictions. Apparently, (long before the Vikings though) for ceremonies, the Norse priests would wear them quite often. Which, I suppose, it's possible that this is where we got the idea for them in the first place.

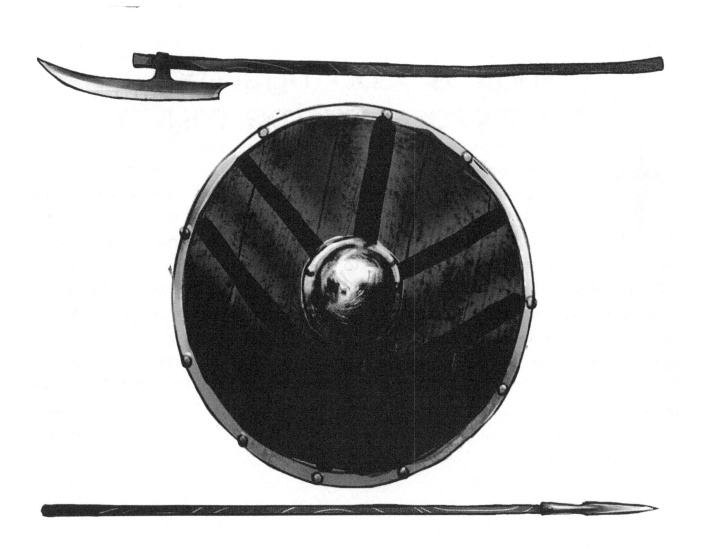

Week Three: "The Fab Four"
A Few Days on Writing Style

So far, you have finished a slew of different writing prompts. As this course continues, I will attempt to not deviate too far from what we have been talking about so you might be able to gain an even greater grasp on the subject at hand. In order to draw out your true ability, I will need to turn up the heat a bit. This week will be about a variety of different subjects. Ideally, it is to test how many facets you can think in. I wouldn't want you to get stuck thinking in only one writing style. You might, then, never unearth what your true potential is!

Day Eleven:
"Expository"

Every writer in this world has their own personal style, ideas, and viewpoints, which cause them to think and write the way that they do. Although this may definitely be so, there are four overall branches which writing will categorically fall under. This week will be an overview of them all.

VOCABULARY: Remember, you should still be writing every word's definition in the back of this book. You should also continue to make and practice the flashcards for words you don't know yet. Your stack might be getting bigger, but so will your vocabulary.

Clutch
Constitute
Esteem
Stun

CHALLENGE:

Today we will be focusing on the expository writing style. Expository is all about giving information from a less than personal point of view. It is to tell someone how something works or what something is. In expository, *do not* talk about how something makes you feel or how it is causing you to think, simply tell us the whys, whats, hows, whos, whens, wheres, and whoms.

Example: There is a lagoon back home that separates the mainland of Florida from Merritt Island, the town wherein I once lived. I drove over the lagoon almost every day; for much of what I needed to do was located on the other side. Whether it was driving to work with my friend after being picked up each morning or driving to someone's house for a night of cards, nothing could keep me from traveling there on a regular basis.

This example is a boring one, but I believe it gets the point across. It's to give out information; but there is no need that it be robotic.

1. Choose one of the following prompt suggestions:
   a) Wilderness Survival Guide.
   b) School Survival Guide.
   c) How to Slay a Dragon.
   d) How to Do a Back Flip.
   e) How to Fly a Plane.
   f) Where You Live.
   g) Where You Work and What You Do There.
   h) How to Cook (Insert Recipe).
   i) Why People Fall in Love.
2. It must be twelve or more sentences.
3. It can be purely comedic, you do not have to be serious.
4. Use at least one metaphor/simile.

Have fun with it.... In fact, don't be boring or you get an F!

viking

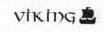

Day Twelve:
"Persuasive"

Do you recall when I first spoke on rhetoric? I had said that we would be mostly speaking on that which pertains to prose. Prose, as you probably well know, represents the branch constituting the average spoken language. It is without guidelines for rhythmic elements, i.e. that of verse and poetry. We will now fix our gaze on the second of the four writing styles. This is the art of persuasion. The ancient predecessors of our modern culture lived, moved, and made their beings using the art of persuasion. Often, in public discourses, you would find men professing their ideals before the congregants of society. They would use whatever graphic models and reasoning they could to evoke a feeling and/or a logical conclusion for the hearers. Arguments would either be won or lost depending on who it was that did the contending. It really is not far from today. Now we advertise, debate amongst ourselves (both in friendliness and contention), recommend, and complain about others. There truly is not an end to what man will do to prove his point. For the most part, each debate is built on a few bases [bey-seez] (plural of basis). Such bases are commonly modeled after the structure of what we would call a syllogism.

A syllogism is a deceptive or deductive argument that looks and sounds a lot like this, "All A is C; all B is A; therefore all B is C*. One version of the syllogism is called the enthymeme. The enthymeme is also often called *the truncated syllogism.* It means it is a short and concise stated reason as to why something is a certain way or as to why one is correct in their hypothesis. The art of persuasion is based off of two separate, yet coinciding, leverage points. They are logos and pathos.

Both logos and pathos are cognate to Greek. Logos deals strictly with the logic of something (i.e. why something is the way that it is) and the solid evidence behind it. Pathos deals with the emotions. It is attempting to cajole or charm someone in such a way as to arouse pity, fear, hate, or even love and approval. There is an inexhaustible well-spring of information on this subject, but, for now, we do not have a reason to delve into it all. Suffice it to say that, if you want to go further on, there are definitely ways you can and without difficulty.

VOCABULARY:
- Assortment
- Expression
- Grimace
- Nimble
- Partisan

CHALLENGE:
Your prompt for today is to convince me. In fifteen sentences or more, pick something that you believe to be entirely and critically worthy to be emphasized; something indispensable that I just "have to" know the details of.

a) You must use whom at least once.
b) You must use all of the daily words.
c) Use at least one metaphor/simile.
d) Don't forget to check for definition accuracy. A wrongly used word can lose the argument

*Description of debate tactic taken from dictionary.com

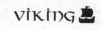

Day Thirteen:
"Narrational"

So, you should already be familiarized with narratives. After all, you probably used this style when you finished the story on Asger. It's simple. There are actually several different ways you can narrate. They all have to do with your perspective.

To start it off, we have:

1. **First Person:** This view is when the narration is from the protagonist's position. What he sees is what you see. How he feels is how you feel. It is very much about what happens next. Even though it is useful, it is still limiting. There is only so much detail you can give the audience when you only have one person to work with. On the other hand, it is a very personal style and people relate well to a character that is as limited as they are.

2. **Second Person:** This is when you speak to the audience directly. It is not really used unless it is for persuasive or expository. Since what I am doing now is expository, it works. For storytelling however, you should probably keep your point of view as first or third person.

3. **Third person:** Here you are using he, she, it, or they. This is possible, although not always advised, for stories. Third person can seem distant and limited in the personal experience realm of the character. Although, it is still a doable option. There is one aspect of third person which I prefer above the rest, it is the third person omniscient.

4. **Third Person Omniscient:** While still considered third person, you are able to identify with what each character is thinking and doing. It gives the entire story a twist where we don't only hear what the main character is doing, but everyone else that is in the story (the enemies, friends, sisters, brothers, even the mother-in-laws) is open to our eyes! I have used this viewpoint. Although, I have found (like with the story of Asger) that first person is very useful. If you notice, at the very end of the story though, once Asger is finished with his elaboration, I switch to third person to describe his actions thereafter.

	Subjective:		Objective:	
1st – I		We	1st – Me	Us
2nd – You		You	2nd – You	You
3rd – He, She, It		They	3rd – Him, Her, It	Them

VOCABULARY:
Dismal

Inquisitive

Pry

Relief

Turret

CHALLENGE:
I will give you several prompts to choose from. You will need to write a story from the perspective of a narrator. You are at liberty to choose your point of view.

1. Prompts:
   a) A fish lost at sea away from his school.
   b) A person who is out to conquer the mountains in their backyard (a place they have always found terrifying).
   c) A bird that is flying to Florida for the summer.
   d) A blacksmith and his journey to becoming recognized by the king.
   e) Twins, one which is evil and the other with a conflicted conscience (either one's perspective will work for the story).
   f) A Native American shaman and their journey for the truth.
   g) A samurai who has been betrayed.
   h) A captain whose ship has been boarded by pirates (could be any time period in history).
   i) An assassin who is conflicted when ordered to kill his best friend.
   j) An Eskimo who goes on an unexpected journey.
   k) A scientist who wants to invent something that no one ever has.
2. You must use whom at least once.
3. It must be fifteen sentences or more.
4. You must use all of the words of the day.
5. Have a good resolution.
6. Have some dialogue (if even just the protagonist's own thoughts).

As always, have fun with it!

Day Fourteen:
"Descriptive"

    The allusively, sly feline's eyes transfixed upon the diminutive, space gray rodent before him, vigorously leaped in order that he might waylay his escaping and, thereby, cutting short his mousy existence. The sentence you just read is an example of descriptive writing. Instead of being boring and saying something like *the cat attacked the mouse*, I said what the cat was like, how intent the cat was, what color the mouse was, how powerfully the cat jumped, and with what vigor. So too, I described why he jumped, and the desired result from it.

    The sentence about the cat and mouse may work, but on average I try to stay away from that many adjectives and adverbs. A story does not need to consist entirely of amplifiers. There is a time and a place for everything. There is a time to give solid facts, a time to coax, a time to tell fantasy, and then there is that oh so desired moment (which, occurring only every so often) to become the gateway for one's craved elaboration. It is at such an occasion that the utterance of his or her pen is transfigured to be as smooth as sterling silver. I do hope that I got my point across. In a way, it is actually easier to garb your words with flowers and spices and to make them sound sweet to the hearer, than to give facts and reasons. It is harder to make an expository sentence sound aesthetically pleasing, than to portray a sunset with its graceful hues of gold and pink. Now, granted, I speak from a very biased position; it is in my nature to try and paint with my words, not to inform with them. As I mentioned before, I do not intend for you to write an exorbitant amount of verbiage. Such sentences are harmful and pedantic. You may possibly need to moderate your modifiers a bit. After all, abstruse stories are sad stories.

    I expected that this week would show you which writing style best suits you and your personality. I have met many people in my travels, and I can truthfully tell you that not a single one was identical to another. There are those that have similar characteristics, but never are they perfectly symmetrical in all their likes, dislikes, inclinations, habits, or predispositions. Therefore, I expect that the writing style of each individual will be just as prone to uniqueness as their personality is. We each are our own type of genius, and I believe that if we were to find that out, there would be far less frustration in the realm of arts and sciences (or just in general). Countless hours and tax dollars would not have to be put toward standard school subjects, which benefit no one. Please don't assume I am saying that it is wrong that we take someone who is not the next Einstein, and give him an education in mathematics. The fact that it is all standardized, that's the issue. Many people will count someone an ignorant fool if they do not attain to the same magnitude of specific smartness as others do. When, all along, that same person, whom they counted an ignorant fool in math and science, has the capability to do so much more than anyone ever gave them credit for. After all, "Everybody is a genius. But if you judge a fish by its ability to climb a tree, it will live its whole life thinking it is stupid." -Albert Einstein. But I digress (a lot actually). Where was I? Oh yes! I was in the middle of discovering your specific style. I do hope this helped with that.

VOCABULARY:

Expose
Frivolity
Incorrect
Intentions
Presume

CHALLENGE: Today might be a fun experience for a lot of you, yet it might be like pulling teeth for others. Not everyone is a poet by nature, which is exactly what creative writing is. Your next objective is to write a slew of descriptive sentences using today's vocabulary words. One thing I do not bring up nearly enough, yet is especially pertinent to this specific situation, is the fact that you need to check (or at least stop and think about) whether the words you use are appropriate for what you want to describe. It is very easy to write a word and not even take the time to see whether it actually makes sense or not. I highly suggest you arrange for yourself a few moments to do so.

1. Prompt suggestions:
    a) Whatever you desire, go for it. Look around you or within yourself; pull your thoughts out! Whatever annoyance is burning a hole in your chest, this is your chance to dowse it. It could be as simple as a journal entry, which you want to elaborate on, or it could be your best attempt at recounting the way the tree in your front yard looks in the winter as opposed to in the spring. It is up to you. You are the master here. Take the wheel.
2. You must use whom and proper subjective pronoun placement when it comes time.
3. Sixteen sentences or more are required.
4. Try to tell a story or relay information (empty words benefit no one). Just make sure you do it in a colorful way.
5. Always look for a better way to say something, even if it sounds good to begin with.
6. Use the daily words.

Have fun, stop being so serious :).

Day Fifteen:
"A Boring Day"

VOCABULARY: Don't forget to memorize old words, and make new cards. Continually reviewing words (even the words that you already know well) will help you to use those words in your everyday life. These memorization exercises are for you to use the words as much as they are for you to know their definitions.

Dismiss
Naught
Resentful
Unwise
Withhold

CHALLENGE: I have decided that today, seeing as you have done so much all week, should be easy. No new material to learn, nothing to read, and no strain. Just a simple warm-up and then you can go on break... or whatever you do when you aren't doing this mission.

1. Use a different writing style for each vocabulary word.
2. You choose which style of writing for each word.
3. Each entry must be three sentences or more.
4. Each entry must contain a synonym of the initial vocabulary word.

I guess that's it. You're dismissed.

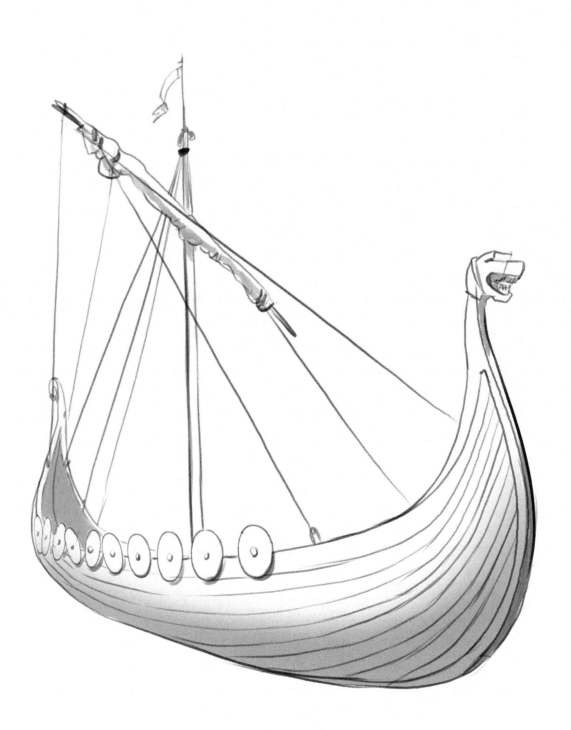

"Linguistic Alteration" The Ancients' Influence

We, as a culture, owe much more to the Vikings than what's found in archeology alone. Through all the raids accomplished by them over time, the intermingling of people led to intermingling of language. The Old Norse and the Old English became amalgamated, which led English to become even more adulterated than it may have already been. Language is always changing and, should we be around for another two thousand years, (let's hope we are not) language as we know it will be utterly and entirely unrecognizable. People, then, will be looking back at today noting the differences and changes throughout.

Week Four: "The Tale of an Anglo"
A Missing Chapter

Realistically speaking, we really don't know much about Asger at all. The upbringing we are given for him is rather ambiguous. But the person, whom we haven't any information on at all, is the antagonist of our story. He is the elusive and wicked brother, whose name is still a mystery to this day. (Unless you gave him one.) I was going to leave it alone, but I came to have a notion. It is the idea that *you* are to be the one to tell the untold tale of the brother. The background of the Anglo-Saxon king will no longer be in the shadows. Please do not jump into this all willy-nilly. This is a very important task. You must approach it with sobriety and respect, for he is not a character to be trifled with. He, too, grew up in dark times, where the weather was harsh, and the master was harsher.

Give the graphic details of his betrayal and of his madness. Cause me to see what led to his eventual downfall. Use whatever type of colorful language you want! In fact, it doesn't even have to be a written story. If I am to encourage creativity, then there can be no bounds. You may write a poem, a very long epic with several verses, each line building upon the next. Such might seem a little intimidating, but if you have experience in this sort of thing, perhaps this is the route you want to take. All that being said, I'm sure whatever you choose will be excellent. Explore, be imaginative. The sky is your limit! This is the project you will be working on all week, starting today. So each day, take time to write some, edit some, fuss over some, and make it perfect for your eyes. You are your own standard, just like when you wrote the ending for Asger. What you might want to do first is explain his background in the Scandinavian Mountains. From there, you might want to add something about Asger, but this is all your own planning.

GUIDELINES:

1. Story must be one page at the very least (give or take a few lines. It doesn't have to be exact).
2. Plan your work.
3. Work your plan.

NOTE 1: Just as with Asger, you will find blank journal pages at the end of this week's section so that you have room to write. There are also pages with each day so that you can write out your warm-ups. You may still use other sources of paper or type your story instead if you prefer, but the pages are there if you want them.

NOTE 2: Remember to continue using all of the day's words in each warm-up, and write the definitions for all words in the back of the book. Also, don't forget to make, and practice your flashcards. The better you know a word, the more you can use it in your writing.

Day Sixteen:
"Of Trees"

VOCABULARY:
    Advocate
    Disclose
    Obtain
    Regain
    Vexed

WARM-UPS: Use all of today's words in both entries.
1. Describe your favorite tree in one hundred words or more (descriptive).
2. Write a second entry, this time an exposition (expository style), on the same tree. Use one hundred words or more.

CHALLENGE: Now get started with your story on Asger's brother! Remember to have fun with it. Be creative (and, if you must, graphic).

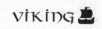

Day Seventeen:
"Birthday Cake and Fools"

VOCABULARY:
- Childish
- Defer
- Revive
- Supplications

WARM-UPS: Use the daily words in both entries (supplications is bound to be a tough one to fit in).
1. Persuade me, in a hundred words or more, as to whether or not I should eat birthday cake for each meal.
2. Tell me, in a hundred words or more, a story about a lolly-gagging fool, who continuously gets in trouble by his boss. Make sure to have a good resolve for it. Make it in either 1st, 2nd, 3rd, or omniscient person.

CHALLENGE: Continue your writing escapade. I'm sure it is turning out swimmingly.

viking

Day Eighteen:
"Dessert Please"

VOCABULARY:
- Apprehend
- Nonetheless
- Scale
- Support
- Vengeance

WARM-UPS: Each entry should be one hundred words or more. Use the words of the day in your description/exposition.
1. Describe the way your favorite dessert tastes and smells. (Be as descriptive as possible.)
2. Describe how you think you would make your favorite dessert.

CHALLENGE: It is time again to write down more of your story. Remember to edit a lot. A helpful hint is waiting a day before you look at what you just wrote. When you look too long at what you just wrote, your judgment can become cloudy. Sometimes, all it takes is a hiatus of varied length for you to see your mistakes. Things are not always going to be crystal clear.

Day Nineteen:
"Nashville and the Force"

VOCABULARY:
    Countless
    Galore
    Noble
    Sorrow

WARM-UPS: Use the words of the day in both entries. Both entries should be at least one page long.
1. Two options:
    a) Persuade me to join the dark or light side of the force.
        i.) If you do not know what the dark or light side is, then look it up on Google or ask your parents, kids, or anyone else.
    b) Persuade me as to why I should not hunt endangered black rhinos for their horns.
2. Tell me a story about a girl who goes to Nashville to live her dream as a country star (singer).

CHALLENGE: Write more of your story.

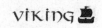

Day Twenty:
"The Tortoises Defense"

VOCABULARY:
- Avenge
- Knelt
- Pact

WARM-UPS: This warm-up may be a little complicated, but it'll be really cool if you can figure it out and do it. So, your mission is to:
1. Tell a story using all four writing styles. It will be a descriptive narration about a rabbit (the judge) and a tortoise (the defendant). The tortoise needs to persuade the judge, and those hearing, that he is innocent. The cops involved are wolves. Give information about why everything is happening (expository).
2. Use three hundred words or more.
3. Intermingle the words of the day within your story and use any synonyms you can find.

CHALLENGE: Today is the day that you should be finishing your story. If you need more time, then give yourself more time. Edit, if you must, for a few more hours. This is all according your liking and not mine. I'm sure that if you have done everything I assigned in this book, you have at the very least gained a larger understanding of writing and its relevance to rhetoric. We will have more of these challenges in the future, but for now, just enjoy the work you have done.

STORY JOURNAL

Here are some pages to work on your story of the brother's history. The last couple of pages are there for you to rewrite your story after you have finished writing and editing it.

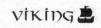

viking

viking

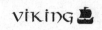

viking

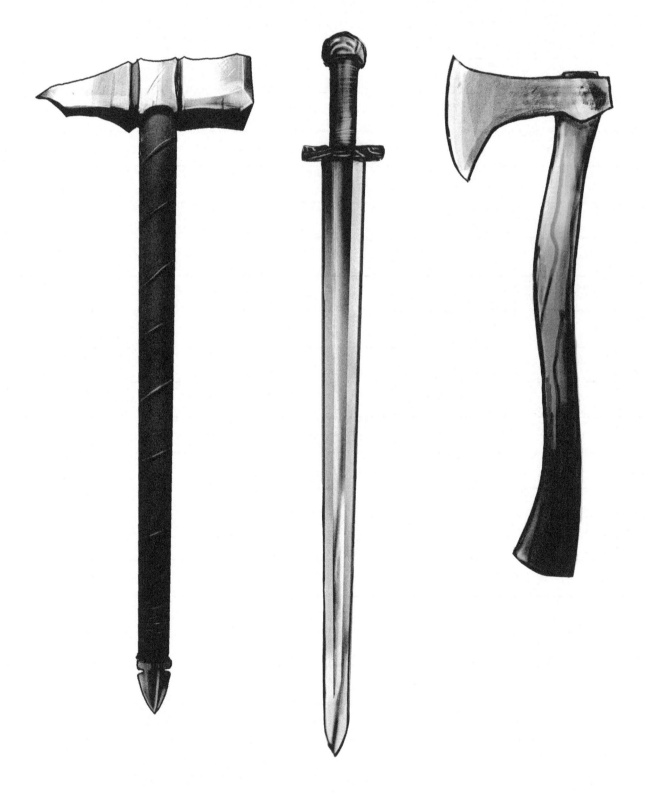

"The Toughest Norseman" on Weapons, Warfare, and Defense

As well as being used for offense, Viking weaponry was used for other things, such as ceremonies and shows of authority. Much of their weaponry was comprised of axes, spears, bows, and (most importantly) swords. Swords, however, were more expensive and difficult to make. They were given, most often, to those who were of higher rank. As far as their defenses went, they had helmets, chain mails, round shields, you name it! Bucklers, (shields) about a meter in length, were sometimes painted with simple colors. Other times, they were painted with pictures of the sagas and legends of Viking mythology and stories told in their day.

Week Five: "Journaling"
Therapy for Writers

If you struggle with writing, welcome to the club. It is indeed a difficult thing to do. Don't get me wrong, it is simple to put words down on a piece of paper; anyone can do it. But to put those words in such a way that is easy for people to understand and enjoy, is hard. How many of you breathed a sigh of relief when I said that? Perhaps you thought you were the only one who thought so. Well, I can say, with all surety, that you are not. Oftentimes, (more than not) I find myself staring at a blank canvas of paper without any idea of what to do next. In fact, when I did my research for these lessons, I came across different grammarian pages that named this exact problem that I run into on a daily basis, as well as other bad habits I need to correct. I found that no matter how far anyone thinks they have gone, they can always go further.

I first realized in high school that something inside of me was drawn to this particular subject. Because for me, more than for the other kids, writing was not arduous. In fact, it made sense. It wasn't that I was a million miles ahead of everyone or that I had an incredibly special gift. I just had a desire and an inclination to learn. I began to enjoy what I did because I could describe my emotions and expound on my beliefs. Whenever I was in "the pits of sorrow", I found it easier to express myself through the pen.

After high school, I forgot everything I knew about stories, essays, and whatnot. I continued, though, to write poetry throughout the next six years, yet only as a hobby. Now, I admit that not all of my poems were (how the kids would say) on point. But, they were spoken from the heart and, often, while I was in a less than favorable place emotionally. If I could find where all of my poems are stored, I'm ninety percent sure that I would laugh at them and probably kick myself over the numerous amounts of grammatical errors within each. This is the extent of my experience. I hope that you can take that as an encouragement. After all, some do not like it when their teacher shows weakness. However, I find that, in life, the best teacher is the one that comes alongside their students, lifts them up and says, let's do this together. All that to say, please do not feel any lesser if you have trouble wrapping your mind around this thing we call *writing*. Believe me, if it were easy, everyone would do it. The very fact that it is difficult, makes it all the more enjoyable when people tell you that you are doing a good job! So please, by all means, continue on. It is an honorable practice.

Many jobs, as well, will consider it an indispensable requirement that you be a skilled writer. What I will give you for the next week is a set of different tips that, should you practice them continuously, will cause you to become a talented writer. It's not like I will be giving you anything that has not been discovered by others. They are not my own ideas (as if there was anything new underneath the sun). Don't think, though, that this means you will not be doing anything all week. I would like you to continuously create. You should constantly practice your skills if you intend to actually get anywhere. The masterpiece, which you will make, is a two page descriptive on any abstract issue/concept within your heart or in your life. The definition of abstract goes as follows: a concept or issue that is not a concrete reality or object.

Example:

"It would be my greatest pleasure to make a loud proclamation about my great admiration of the substance we call food. It might be a strange thing to say, yet definitely not an untruth. The aroma of freshly baked cookies, the supplications my stomach composes when an illustrious turkey is presented before me, and the terse ding the oven generates when the time of resolution has come, are all experiences which resound forth in my memory whenever my stomach has decided it is time to devour. But, aside from that, I am just about head over heels for any chance I get to virtually consume my entire body weight. Especially when dealing with the glories of lasagna. My eyes are yet to behold a meal which does not please them. If I am to be entirely honest though, my passion for food is possibly, maybe, probably, most likely a bit inordinate. Just don't tell my doctor. Truly though, what can I say? I burn weight even while I sleep. Plus, seemingly constant workouts do not help me to do otherwise."

The abstract subject in the example was love and how he felt about eating. Food is concrete (meaning it's a solid object and not a concept or thought process). It also talks about how he could tell that his habits and thought processes may have been off a little (in reality, a lot). The above is a very unserious depiction of what I am trying to exemplify. I simply do not, at the moment, have it in my being to write on a serious subject. Think of it as if you were writing in a journal about your own thoughts. I have just eaten a very large meal, ergo, I wrote about food. You can be as open and bare as you want. Although, it has to have correct grammar and contextually correct wordage. You have the entire week to finish the assignment and it must be two pages at the very least. Again, there are pages for you at the back of this week's section. So, get back to writing!

Day Twenty-One:
"More on Reading"

One thing I did not stress near as strongly as I should have, was the importance of reading. Whomever you wish to write like, whether they are your favorite author or your favorite blogger, you must examine their material (and a lot of it at that) if you ever hope to write as well as they do. I assume that you have placed this on your to do list, but if you have not, it is never too late to start. Make sure that you do not study anyone's work that is below your level, unless that author is talking to the particular age group you are interested in. Albeit the case, you should probably read the sort of books which cause you to scratch your head due to the collective usage of vocabulary throughout.

Now that you have heard what I have to say, I suggest that you wait ne'er a moment longer. Obtain these books of which I speak. Search them out, especially classics. The Odyssey is a good one to check out. 'Where the Red Fern Grows', 'A Land Remembered', 'Les Miserables' are all great choices as well. Books are literally everywhere. If you think that you can get away with being a writer while not examining other people's works, then you have another thing to consider. I know some may have a difficult time with this. I understand your frustration completely. It is not the easiest thing to do, especially if you are prone to random sleep fits as I am. I cannot tell you the number of places people have found me passed out (usually with a book prostrated across my face). At one point, they contemplated dedicating a picture collage in my honor. Needless to say, it is still one thing you should never neglect.

VOCABULARY:

Deserted
Dishearten
Heavily
Imagine
Spontaneity

WARM-UP: Don't forget to use today's words.
1. Write eight separate sentences using alliteration.
    a) Alliteration is when the same letter or sound is at the beginning of each word. Connecting words such as prepositions, articles, etc. are alright to place between adjectives, nouns, and verbs without having letters that match.

2. Be sure to use metaphors and similes if you can.

CHALLENGE: Now get to working more on your journal entry!

Day Twenty-Two: "Avert from Superfluities"
Don't Overdo It

We all know that adjectives and adverbs are fun to write. Oftentimes, it can be so easy just to say the first thing that comes to your head. Throughout this entire book, I'm sure you were able to rattle off multitudes of various words without any sort of issue at all. Although, we are inclined to think of this as a good stratagem, it may actually take away from the message you are attempting to convey. You must understand me in this. It is not an awful thing to write adjectives and adverbs; they are there for a reason. But, what I have learned is that we as authors need not overload our sentences with every single intensifier in the book. Stories that contain such material tend to just come off as pretentious and good for nothing. They do not at all edify the person listening. Metaphors are another thing that can place a burden or a strain on your story. These tools are not intrinsically evil, but they have the potential to corrupt an otherwise fantastic story.

E.g.:The prodigious, bear-like barbarian effortlessly overwhelmed the substantial battalion with but his defenseless, naked palms, unattended was he by any other alternative advocates.

This is an example of intensifiers used much too liberally. Anyone can construct a sentence like this. All you must do is type up something plain, take all the average words, and alter them to whatever you can find in the thesaurus, and voila! You have a grade A trash sentence. You may wonder what you should do then to compose reasonably vivacious word play without the unnecessary air of pretense. With all this I have said, you may even doubt your authenticity as a writer, but fear not. Know that there is more than one way to cut an apple. In order to take all the distraction and clutter away, one of only a few things you must do is find a better *verb* to substitute both the adjective/adverb and the connecting noun. You may need to rearrange your entire statement/question in order that it does not sound clumsy. This is much harder to do, but it is worth it. Most of all, it is achievable. Try to limit yourself to a total of only two to four adjectives a paragraph. The same principle should go for adverbs as well.

E.g.:The brute, without so much as a weapon, yet with a strong hand, annihilated the opposing forces unto oblivion. There were none nearby to succor; albeit he needed them not.

VOCABULARY:
Conclude
Flee
Groan
Inhabitant
Obvious

WARM-UPS: Use your words.
1. Write five separate sentences with boring vocabulary.
2. Then, replace the words with a dizzying amount of synonyms, adjectives, and adverbs.
3. Once you are done with #2, figure out a way to rearrange the words entirely. This time, you will be using a suitable balance of everything.

CHALLENGE: It is now time for you to continue with your journaling. May the force be with you.

Day Twenty-Three: "The Importance of Grammar"
Seek Perfection, Find Excellence

Some of you may have wondered why I had you go through all of the grammar rules before I gave you the opportunity to write a lot. Well, first of all, your material (whether you like it or not) is going to be, at some point, viewed by others who have prejudices about those exact things we went over. I, myself, am a very jaundiced individual whose eyes will glide across sentence after sentence. Most of the time, I'm not even giving two cents about what is actually said within them, but I pick the grammar to death. Therefore, now that I've made my case, know that grammar *should not* be a standard, which tells if you are a creative and talented individual. However, many are not able to enjoy the content of a paper if it's an entire mess. I suggest you search these things out. Don't worry; this is not going to be a lesson where I express a whole bunch of different mistakes made by most of the population. Let's suffice it to say that if you are interested to find out what you may or may not be doing wrong, I'll allow you to take it upon your own shoulders to better your understanding. After all, there are many others far better than I who are able to expound much further and much more efficiently. I wish you happy hunting.

VOCABULARY:

Anxious
Excellent
Tax
Whereabouts
Yearn

WARM-UPS:
1. Look up Jon Gingerich's article about the top twenty grammar mistakes on Google.
2. Write three sentences with boring grammar.
3. Spruce those sentences up through the use of the thesaurus.
4. Then, attempt to undo any poorness therein by making them sound satisfying.
5. Don't forget to use the daily vocabulary

CHALLENGE: Continue writing your journal entry.

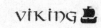

VIKING

Day Twenty-Four: "Gerunds and Boring Endings"
Don't Put People to Sleep

There are many killers to a good story. Perhaps, one of the things which will best put a reader to sleep is the overuse of words ending with "ing". This is known as a boring verb end-ing by many, and using it in every sentence should be avoided. Some say that one should only include, at the very most, two or three verbs of this type. Such things are not difficult to fix. Although, it may take moving some words around before they actually sound good. If you use verbs with these endings too often, it will create a drag on your story and lose people's interest.

Example: I am having a guest that is staying at my house. She tends to be hitting a lot of issues while dealing with her associates. Her accumulating of said issues is driving me crazy! I am hoping that she settles this annoying acquiring ASAP.

As Opposed To: I have a guest here at my house. During her stay, she has accumulated many issues with certain associates of hers. These issues are bound to eventually drive me insane. I have hopes that she settles them all soon so that I may get some rest.

A gerund is a verb that has been altered into a noun. You are able to do this by taking an -ing and affixing it to the end of the verb.

Example: His making was accomplished after he had gone through heavy trials. Such is alright to do as long as you stay away from using it too often.

VOCABULARY:
Embroider
Keen
Ominous
Overtaken

WARM-UPS:
1. Correct these sentences:
   a) Many are constantly looking fervently for loving.
   b) Few truly are finding what they are looking for.
   c) If they were instead attempting more to be searching for what is important, then in the process, they would eventually, magnificently come to what they were wanting in the first place.
2. Write ten or more sentences about a lizard that falls into a toxic waste dump and becomes a terrorizing monster.

CHALLENGE:
Now, continue with your journal entry. If you have already finished, then you could even start a new one if you want.

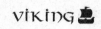

Day Twenty-Five:
"The Passive Voice"

It is not the Dread of Society. The *passive voice* is a very misunderstood subject. I have heard, and even been a part of, conversations where the main point was how to tell or know what it actually is and whether it is ok to use. Although, we tried our hardest to figure it out, we missed the target by a long shot.

Many would suggest that it is unfavorable to use the passive voice altogether. There are those who would even turn purple with what I am about to say next. It is *not* bad to use it, and it's sometimes even needed. Please, put the pitch forks and torches back in your sheds. The world will continue to spin. You may not even know its true definition. You may believe that you are eschewing it with all your might. I will try my best to put it into perspective and explain it with all the accuracy possible. I assume you remember the definitions of the *subjective case* and the *objective case*. You must know these first for it is crucial for you to understand the passive voice. If you did in fact forget their meaning, then I suggest you go back to week one, and read the article I have already written on them.

The opposite of the passive voice is the *active voice*. These two are the only voices we have in the English language. To describe these two as briefly as possible, the Active Voice is when the *subject* of the sentence is doing the action, and the passive voice is when the subject is being acted upon by the object.

Example:
Active: Ronny hates the circus.

Passive: The circus is hated by Ronny.

The first example is Ronny in the Active; the second is Ronny in the Passive. Either way, Ronny hates the circus; the only difference is that he changes cases. Both sentences are acceptable and can be used if needed. There are definitely times when one should not use the passive voice. It can often lead to someone being too wordy. Or, when attempting to make a sentence work in the Passive, it can lead to someone making grammatical errors. Other than situations where it cannot be used, there are the plethora of times where it is entirely fine and perhaps even needed. Use your discretion. Also know, though, that the active voice is preferred and will most likely be of greater use to you when writing an action thriller. I implore you to dig further into this subject. Take your time to search these things out, to memorize them, and to master them. They may be your next stepping stone to being the writer that you want to be.

VOCABULARY:
    Excessive
    Frigid
    Impulse
    Launching
    Rage

WARM-UPS:

1. Reorganize these sentences so that the object is the subject:

   a) The gang fight was promptly ended by the police.

   b) The sky king was greatly amused by the feast which was brought before him.

   c) The little boy thought it not necessary that he come in for dinner that night, thereby causing his parents to worry for his safety.

   d) The world spins on an axis because it is acted upon by an unseen force.

   e) Engulfed in fire, the man decided that he would never return to the pizzeria again.

   f) The water became frozen when it was touched by an icy finger.

2. Today's warm-up is a little different from the others, but still try using the words of the day in your sentences.

CHALLENGE:
Today is the day that you should be finished with your journal entry. If you are not, then finish it whenever you can.

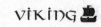

VIKING

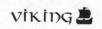

"Not Something to be Unsure About"

The Afterlife in Norse Mythology.

There is no dogmatic forth giving of where they, as a culture, believed they would go when they died. In fact, there are a plethora of different levels which are referenced all throughout Norse mythology and sagas alike. The most popular is probably one you have already guessed. Valhalla is the place wherein warriors believed they would go when they died in battle. It was for this reason that they were not afraid when they went off to war. Much of what they would do in Valhalla was exactly what they already did on planet earth. (This seems like the perfect place to go for a bunch of already carnal individuals). Different dwelling places for those that passed away included a place called Folkvang and Hel, none of which is particularly unambiguous. We are forced to infer, as in a mirror dimly. Thankfully, it's not they whom we should take seriously in these sorts of issues.

Week Six: "Final"
Write a Short Story

"What? What do you mean final?" This is what you may have thought to yourself when you saw the title for this week. The rumors are true! Although there may be seven weeks in this book, the final starts now. Don't be frightened by the thought of it. After all, this isn't your ordinary writing course. This is not intended to be drudgery for you. It is for your enjoyment. Writing isn't meant to be overbearing; but to be fun. It can take you into worlds uncreated. It can take you through events unimaginable! Truly, it is a blessing. Who knows when this skill will come in handy? Even if this is not your primary pursuit in life, it is still exceedingly advantageous that you learn at least the basics.

Over the next two weeks, you will be undertaking the task of creating your very own short story, about your very own topic of choice. You have the liberty to write it about whomever you wish and in whichever time period you desire.

The Guidelines:

1. If typed, it must be no shorter than two pages and no longer than two and a half pages.
    a) It should be size 12 in a standard font
    b) If you use dyslexie, you should use size 8.
2. If writing by hand, then it should be three standard pages long. (As always, there are pages provided at the end of this week's section.)

Write it to the caliber of publish-worthy material. Imagine that at the end of the course, your story will be seen by millions. This assignment will be the culmination of what you have learned over the past five weeks. Rest assured that if you continue with your writing hereafter, the only things needed will be a passion to learn and a love for what you do. Should you have those two things, you WILL grow to be an incredible author indeed. Stretch yourself on this paper. Think outside the worn out box you may have created for yourself. I trust this is exactly what you have been doing during your time with this book.

Things to consider:

1. Write a captivating first sentence + first paragraph.
2. Choose whether you will write it in 1st, 2nd, or 3rd person.
3. Develop details about your character(s) and who they are.
4. Choose dialogue that is useful and plot inducing.
5. Be descriptive about where your character is and what is around them.
6. Plot is important, include tension.
7. Make a cause for crisis.
8. Resolve everything or leave it open ended (depending on your ruthlessness).

Day Twenty-Six:
"In Memory of Your Childhood"

VOCABULARY:
- Convenient
- Dwell
- Gravity
- Impudence
- Sufficient

WARM-UP:
1. Write for ten minutes about your favorite childhood memory in a descriptive tone.
2. Remember to use today's words in your description.

That's all I have for you. I want you to be ready to get started on your short story. This is your chance to do something incredible.

CHALLENGE: It is time to begin your story.

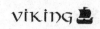

viking

Day Twenty-Seven:
"Unfamiliar Adventuring"

VOCABULARY: Remember to use your words in the warm-ups, to do your definitions, make your flashcards, and practice.

- Alike
- Daze
- Delay
- Sevenfold
- Usage

WARM-UP: Write for ten minutes about what you would do if you ever got to go to a continent you have never been on before. Mention where you would go, what type of food you would look forward to eating, what you would do, etc....

CHALLENGE: Continue writing your short story.

VIKING

Day Twenty-Eight:
"Acumen Not Yet Revealed"

VOCABULARY:
    By-standing
    Graceless
    Pursue
    Trite
    Trivial

WARM-UP: Write for ten minutes about anything important you learned this past year.

CHALLENGE: Continue with your story.

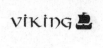

Day Twenty-Nine:
"A Poetic Repose and a Bewildered Awakening"

VOCABULARY:
- Astonishment
- Comparison
- Dodge
- Precise

WARM-UP: Write for ten minutes about a girl who wakes up from a long sleep to find that she is in a different dimension.

CHALLENGE: Onward and upward with your story!

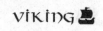

Day Thirty:
"King of the Wolves"

VOCABULARY:
- Blatancy
- Familiar
- Impossible
- Plunge
- Stew

WARM-UP: Write for ten minutes from the perspective of a wolf pack leader. It can be at any time of the year.

CHALLENGE: You should be at least half way done with your story today. Edit at your own liberty.

VIKING

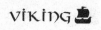

STORY JOURNAL

Here are some pages to work on your very own story. Remember that it can be about anything you choose. Be creative, and let your imagination run free.

viking

VIKING

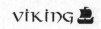

VIKING

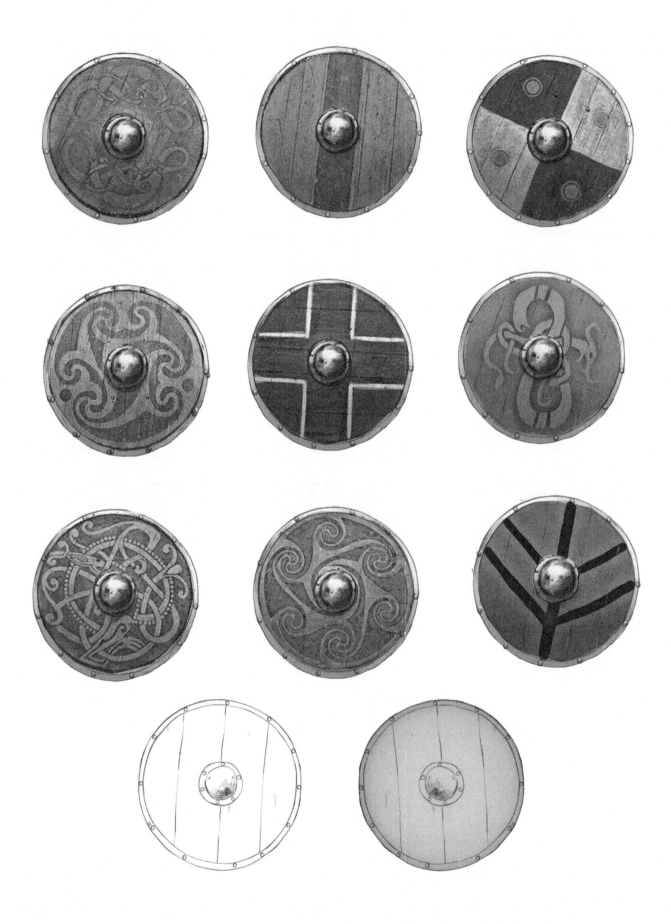

"The Hills are Alive"
The Scandinavians and the Sun

The Scandinavian mountain range constitutes most of Norway and much of Sweden, yet hardly any part of Finland. In this region, the sun probably tends to shine a bit more excessively than where you live. During the summer months, he (like an extrovert) just never wants to shut up. Forcing his way into everyone's business, he spends his time in the sky non-stop. When the winter comes, his introverted side takes control, and he hides himself. Now that I think about it, this tends to be the modus operandi of most of the human beings I know. Needless to say though, the mountains are definitely among the greats, beautiful as all get out, with glaciers abundant and wildlife galore. It's on my bucket list to visit one day. Here's to hoping that such becomes reality.

Week Seven: "Practice Perfects"
Daily Routines

    A very wise man once told me that if I want to be a successful writer, I would need to write for fifteen minutes, every single day. He said, "Do it without hesitation. Just get to the presses. Don't even take breaks to edit." I feel though that very aspect is my largest stumbling block. I have the hardest time containing my impulses to glance back at whatever I am writing. Unhindered writing actually remains an unvisited practice of mine. Although that may be the case, I agree with the experts. Drilling yourself in this area is one of the best things you could ever do. For this reason, I have sought to reinforce within you these very habits. This week I will seek to further ingrain the concept into your mind and heart. I'll be giving you various tasks every day to get you warmed up to finish your short story. You can continue writing the story in the previous section, or you can move your story to the extra journal pages that you'll find at the end of this section.

Day Thirty-One:
"Somnum Pacific"

VOCABULARY:
- Increase
- Logging
- Runaway
- Speedy
- Twang

WARM-UP: Imagine you are telling someone a bedtime story after tucking them in. You look through the deepest part of your mind for whatever you can pull up... then, you open your mouth. For fifteen minutes, elaborate on your story. Don't forget to use your vocabulary words.

CHALLENGE: Keep working on your short story.

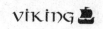

viking

Day Thirty-Two:
"Band Geeks and Guitar Freaks"

VOCABULARY:
- Faithful
- Healing
- Inevitable
- Presence
- Restoration

WARM-UP: For fifteen minutes, write from the perspective of someone in a band. It could be from the perspective of any of the band members.

CHALLENGE: You guessed it. Keep working on your short story.

VIKING

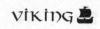

Day Thirty-Three:
"I Found Somethin', Clem!"

VOCABULARY:
- Abate
- Betray
- Stratagem
- Triumph
- Undergo

WARM-UP: Write for fifteen minutes from the perspective of a fisherman who found a treasure at the bottom of a lake on which he fished frequently.

CHALLENGE: Now it is time to get back to your short story. You should be nearly finished. If you are finished, go back through and edit it.

Day Thirty-Four:
"Of Barbie Dolls and Baseball Bats"

VOCABULARY:
- Dormant
- Drift
- Excitement
- Horizon
- Undoubted

WARM-UP: Write for fifteen minutes from the perspective of a five year old at their birthday party.

CHALLENGE: How's that story coming along?

VIKING

viking

Day Thirty-Five:
"Beans, Bacon, Whiskey, and Lard"

VOCABULARY:
- Contrary
- Freeze
- Retreat
- Savage
- Tale

WARM-UP: Write for fifteen minutes from the perspective of an explorer who has found the lost city of Atlantis.

CHALLENGE: You should have finished your short story by now. Do whatever is needed to edit, and finish it up.

viking

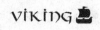

viking

CONGRATULATIONS, you have completed the mission!

The rest of this book is for you to continue writing. Keep learning, growing, and practicing so that you can become a writer as strong with the pen as a Viking warrior with his sword. Keep practicing your flashcards until you have mastered all of the words. Then, find more words to learn. From this point, I bid thee a farewell. I will see you next time.

JOURNAL

VIKING

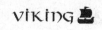

viking

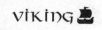

viking

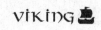

VIKING

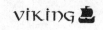

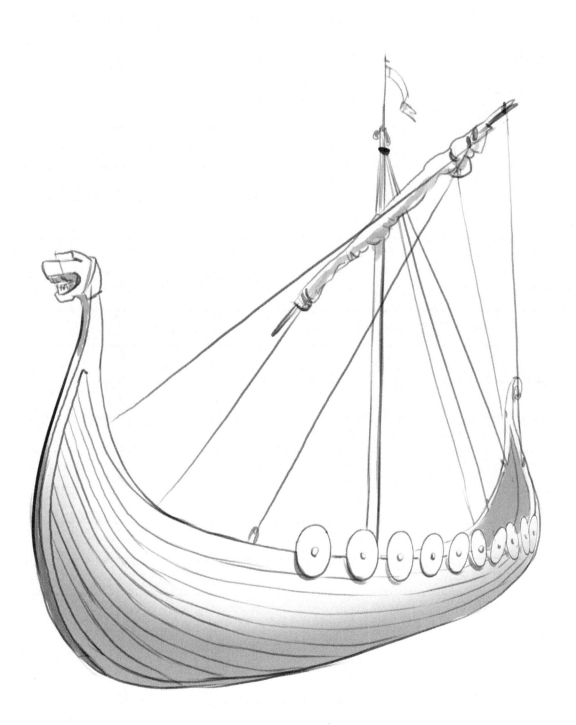

VOCABULARY DEFINITIONS LIST

VIKING

1.) Abate -

2.) Abrupt -

3.) Advocate -

4.) Alike -

5.) Ambush -

6.) Amidst -

7.) Anxious -

8.) Apprehend -

9.) Ascend -

10.) Assortment -

11.) Astonishment -

12.) Avenge -

13.) Bearing -

14.) Betray -

15.) Bitter -

16.) Blatancy -

17.) By-standing -

18.) Chaos -

19.) Childish -

20.) Clamor -

21.) Clutch   -

22.) Comparison -

23.) Conclude   -

24.) Constitute -

25.) Contend   -

26.) Contrary   -

27.) Convenient -

28.) Countless   -

29.) Daze   -

30.) Deem   -

31.) Defer -

32.) Delay -

33.) Deserted -

34.) Deviate -

35.) Disclose -

36.) Dishearten -

37.) Dismal -

38.) Dismiss -

39.) Disown -

40.) Dodge -

41.) Dormant -

42.) Drift -

43.) Dwell -

44.) Elaborate -

45.) Embroider -

46.) Esteem -

47.) Excellent -

48.) Excessive -

49.) Excitement -

50.) Expose -

51.) Expression -

52.) Extermination -

53.) Extreme -

54.) Faithful -

55.) Familiar -

56.) Flee -

57.) Flow -

58.) Foolish -

59.) Former -

60.) Freeze -

VIKING

61.) Frenzy –

62.) Frigid –

63.) Frivolity –

64.) Galore –

65.) Graceless –

66.) Gravity –

67.) Grimace –

68.) Groan –

69.) Healing –

70.) Heavily –

71.) Horizon   -

72.) Imagine   -

73.) Impossible -

74.) Impregnable -

75.) Impudence   -

76.) Impulse   -

77.) Incorrect   -

78.) Increase   -

79.) Inevitable -

80.) Infer -

viking

81.) Inhabitant   -

82.) Inquisitive -

83.) Intense   -

84.) Intensity   -

85.) Intentions   -

86.) Justifiable -

87.) Keen -

88.) Kindle -

89.) Knelt -

90.) Launching -

91.) Logging   -

92.) Magnificent -

93.) Multitude   -

94.) Naught   -

95.) Nimble   -

96.) Noble   -

97.) Nonetheless -

98.) Obtain   -

99.) Obvious   -

100.) Ominous   -

VIKING

101.) Oppose －

102.) Overtaken －

103.) Pact －

104.) Partisan －

105.) Plunge －

106.) Precise －

107.) Presence －

108.) Presume －

109.) Progression －

110.) Pry －

111.) Pulsate -

112.) Pursue -

113.) Rage -

114.) Regain -

115.) Relief -

116.) Resentful -

117.) Restoration -

118.) Retreat -

119.) Revive -

120.) Runaway -

VIKING

121.) Savage -

122.) Scale -

123.) Sevenfold -

124.) Sheer -

125.) Skilled -

126.) Slay -

127.) Sorrow -

128.) Speedy -

129.) Spontaneity -

130.) Stalwart -

131.) Stamina -

132.) Stew -

133.) Stratagem -

134.) Stun -

135.) Sufficient -

136.) Supplications -

137.) Support -

138.) Tale -

139.) Tax -

140.) Trite -

141.) Triumph   -

142.) Trivial   -

143.) Turrent   -

144.) Twang   -

145.) Unbeknownst   -

146.) Undergo   -

147.) Undoubted   -

148.) Unwise   -

149.) Usage   -

150.) Valiant   -

151.) Vengeance - _____
_____

152.) Vexed   - _____
_____

153.) Whereabouts - _____
_____

154.) Withhold   - _____
_____

155.) Yearn   - _____
_____
_____
_____
_____
_____
_____
_____
_____

VOCABULARY WORD LIST

	DAY 1	DAY 2	DAY 3	DAY 4	DAY 5
WEEK ONE		Contend	Chaos	Disown	Amidst
		Elaborate	Deviate	Extermination	Clamor
		Magnificent	Flow	Extreme	Slay
		Multitude	Former	Intense	
		Valiant	Unbeknownst		

	DAY 6	DAY 7	DAY 8	DAY 9	DAY 10
WEEK TWO	Frenzy	Ascend	Ambush	Deem	Abrupt
	Kindle	Bearing	Intensity	Foolish	Bitter
	Pulsate	Impregnable	Justifiable	Oppose	Progression
	Sheer	Infer	Skilled		Stalwart
	Stamina				

	DAY 11	DAY 12	DAY 13	DAY 14	DAY 15
WEEK THREE	Clutch	Assortment	Dismal	Expose	Dismiss
	Constitute	Expression	Inquisitive	Frivolity	Naught
	Esteem	Grimace	Pry	Incorrect	Resentful
	Stun	Nimble	Relief	Intentions	Unwise
		Partisan	Turret	Presume	Withhold

	DAY 16	DAY 17	DAY 18	DAY 19	DAY 20
WEEK FOUR	Advocate	Childish	Apprehend	Countless	Avenge
	Disclose	Defer	Nonetheless	Galore	Knelt
	Obtain	Revive	Scale	Noble	Pact
	Regain	Supplications	Support	Sorrow	
	Vexed		Vengeance		

	DAY 21	DAY 22	DAY 23	DAY 24	DAY 25
WEEK FIVE	Deserted	Conclude	Anxious	Embroider	Excessive
	Dishearten	Flee	Excellent	Keen	Frigid
	Heavily	Groan	Tax	Ominous	Impulse
	Imagine	Inhabitant	Whereabouts	Overtaken	Launching
	Spontaneity	Obvious	Yearn		Rage

	DAY 26	DAY 27	DAY 28	DAY 29	DAY 30
WEEK SIX	Convenient	Alike	By-standing	Astonishment	Blatancy
	Dwell	Daze	Graceless	Comparison	Familiar
	Gravity	Delay	Pursue	Dodge	Impossible
	Impudence	Sevenfold	Trite	Precise	Plunge
	Sufficient	Usage	Trivial		Stew

	DAY 31	DAY 32	DAY 33	DAY 34	DAY 35
WEEK SEVEN	Increase	Faithful	Abate	Dormant	Contrary
	Logging	Healing	Betray	Drift	Freeze
	Runaway	Inevitable	Stratagem	Excitement	Retreat
	Speedy	Presence	Triumph	Horizon	Savage
	Twang	Restoration	Undergo	Undoubted	Tale

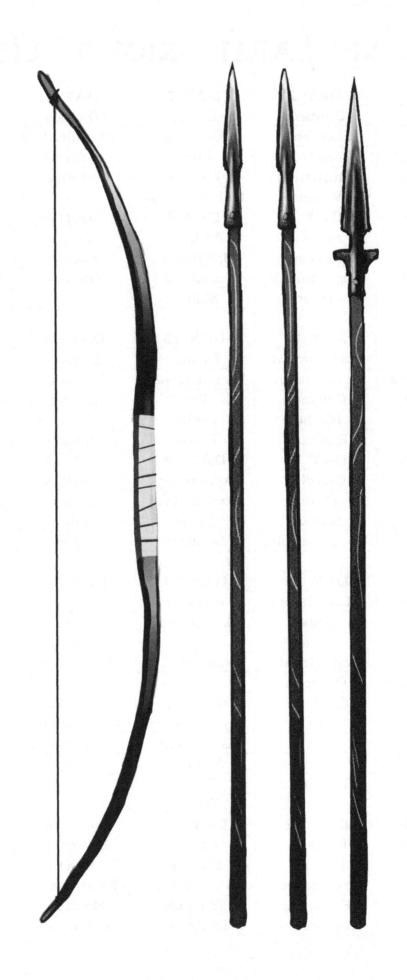

FUNSCHOOLINGBOOKS.COM
THE THINKING TREE PUBLISHING
COMPANY

COPYRIGHT 2017
DO NOT COPY

Made in the USA\
Coppell, TX\
15 April 2024